DATE DUE

JUL 2 8 1991	
MAR 8 1992	
MAR 3 1 1992	
APR 2 0 1992	
NOV 1 9 1992	
JUL 8 1993	
SEP. 2 3 1994	
JAN 2 4 1997	

FLAGS
OF TEXAS

FLAGS
OF TEXAS

By Charles E. Gilbert, Jr.
Illustrated by James Rice

Pelican Publishing Company
GRETNA 1989

First published by Charles W. Parsons, Publisher 1964
Reprinted by Charles W. Parsons, Publisher 1972
Revised edition published by Pelican Publishing Company, Inc. 1989

Pelican edition
First printing, May 1989

Library of Congress Cataloging-in-Publication Data

Gilbert, Charles E. (Charles Edwin), 1888-
  Flags of Texas

  Rev. ed. of: A concise history of early
Texas, c1964.
    1. Flags--Texas--History. 2. Texas--History.
I. Rice, James, 1934-   . II. Title.
CR114.T4G55   1989   929.9'2'09764   88-34511
ISBN 0-88289-721-7

Manufactured in Hong Kong

Published by Pelican Publishing Company, Inc.
1101 Monroe Street, Gretna, Louisiana 70053

Contents

FLAGS OF TEXAS

Preface

Most Texans know well the history of the Lone Star State, but a vast majority of them never tire of listening to its glorious annals. So this book was planned to review the exceptional deeds of the men and women whose valor and perseverance created out of a wilderness this land of opportunity and progress which is Texas today.

The author authentically and chronologically relates in a novel manner the history of this vast area, from the time the first white men set foot upon its rugged and barren shores, up to the beginning of the Civil War. This concise early history of Texas is depicted mainly by the thirty-three colorful flags which played such a vital part in this state's renowned past.

These flags, fully described here, were held high over the heads of undaunted patriots as they marched into battle. The banners did much to make the brave men who were the creators of Texas see their dreams of establishing an independent Texas come true. Not only did these flags inspire those who followed their gay colors and impelling inscriptions, but each has a history that, related chronologically, vividly portrays the establishment of a great state.

That is why, whether a loyal Texan or just someone interested in its unusual history, one should know the important and often spectacular part these flags played in the history of the Lone Star State. For by knowing the history of the Texas flags, you become acquainted with the manner in which the Republic of Texas was established and how this now important area finally became the twenty-eighth state of the United States—a Union of fifty sovereign states.

We have selected this means of presenting the exceptional early history of Texas because the flag, as a symbol of group identification, has been revered and honored since time immemorial.

The first flag known to man was the most awe-inspiring and the most beautiful ever displayed. Possibly this is because it was designed and displayed by God, and brought to a bewildered and harassed world a promise from the King of Kings that life for them would continue. It was more colorful, larger, and more spectacular than mere man, with all his learning and ingenuity, has ever been able to devise. It was the rainbow, a God-sent flag blazing in the skies of a water-soaked world that left only those aboard the Ark alive.

Perhaps from the memory of its beauty and its promise has come the inspiration—and the custom—of all who go forth to battle, to carry high and proudly a flag or banner as a token of their promise of a finer life and a better government. From such inspirations, the flags of nations have become revered as symbols of God's gift of freedom to man.

This intense dedication to the flags so proudly followed in battle is vividly evident in this brief history of the pioneer forefathers of Texas.

FLAGS
OF TEXAS

A Concise History of Early Texas
1519 to 1861

Twenty-seven years after Columbus discovered America, the first white man set foot on the wild and undeveloped land which is now Texas.

In the summer of 1519, Captain Alonzo Alvarez de Pineda, a Spanish explorer who had hope of discovering a new water route to China, sailed his small ship into the Gulf of Mexico. After landing his small force briefly on that sandy beach of what some maintain was Galveston Island, he sailed up and down the Texas coast.

Pineda made a crude map showing the present Texas coastal line and added the locations of the mouths of most of the Texas rivers. History records this map as the first to be made of this part of the United States of today. This map, made 470 years ago, is still a valuable historical paper preserved by the Spanish government. Photographs of it can be viewed in the library of the University of Texas.

Nearly ten years after Pineda skirted much of the Texas coast, another Spanish expedition, commanded by Panfilo de Narvaez, was shipwrecked on an island off the coast, and Alvar Nunez Cabeza de Vaca and several surviving companions lived on the coast for a period of several years.

Cabeza de Vaca was the first European to explore the mainland of Texas. He was the first man to record the early history of this land which is now the Lone Star State, and part of his records have been preserved. Some historians say his Spanish flag of Lions and Castles was the first to be planted on these shores. Other historians believe he carried the colorful flag of the Church of Spain.

FIRST PERMANENT SPANISH SETTLEMENT IN 1682

Many other Spanish expeditions landed on or traversed Texas during the following century, but the Pueblo of Ysleta, a settlement founded in 1682, was the first permanent one made in Texas by the Spanish. Ysleta, about twelve miles from El Paso, is still in existence. A list of the original ninety-odd Spanish families to reside there is still preserved.

The first mission and pueblo in Texas, Corpus Christi de la Ysleta

---

SPANISH MISSIONS

Spain began its building of missions in Texas in 1700 with the founding of Mission San Francisco Solano on the Rio Grande. In 1718, this mission was moved near the Presidio of San Antonio.

The most beautiful of all early Texas missions was San Jose, built in 1720, four miles below San Antonio. The best preserved of all old Texas missions are the five at San Antonio, and of these the most noted is the Alamo.

An early map of Texas outlining colonies of the empresarios

In 1685 La Salle, the noted French explorer, landed in the vicinity of Lavaca Bay and for a short time established a fort and colony near the place where the town of Indianola later stood. He called it Fort St. Louis.

Not until 1716, however, did Spain make a great effort to create a more permanent and sizeable location in Texas, and this East Texas settlement lasted less than two years. In 1718 they did found San Antonio, which for many years was the seat of first the Spanish government in Texas and later the Mexican government there. When the Mexicans were victorious over the Spaniards in 1821, they raised their green, red, and white flag over what is now Texas.

THE ERA OF THE FILIBUSTERS

While many of the early attempts to separate the land of the Tejas from the Spanish—and Mexico—were made by men who sought adventure and excitement, they were also motivated by the growing sentiment of the American people to eliminate from this continent any and all royal authority of the European nations.

Many of the daring attempts of the white men to colonize Texas, related here, were unsuccessful. In many instances the lives of the

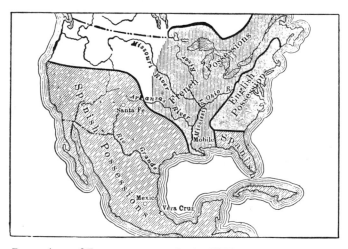

Possessions of European countries in 1700

heroic men were lost, but every failure, every death of a heroic leader was but a stepping-stone to the ultimate victory at San Jacinto which freed the Texans from the Mexican dictator's oppressive reign, and eventually brought into this great Union of States an area which added approximately one-third to its size.

As the part these valiant men played in the creation of Texas is retold, the telling will not only pay a just tribute to their bravery and their daring, but will glorify the wondrous history they did so much to create.

PHILIP NOLAN

Probably the first of these expedition leaders was a buccaneer without a flag—Philip Nolan, a great soldier, scholar, and civil engineer. Born in Ireland, his early manhood was spent in Kentucky. His first trip to Texas, made in 1797, was as a hunter of the wild mustang horses which were numerous at that time on the Texas plains. On his second trip to Texas, however, this time as a leader of a large body of mounted men, he made an unsuccessful attempt to run the Spanish authorities out of Texas. In a fight with troops of the Spanish governor, he was killed and most of his band captured.

ANGLO-AMERICAN HOMESTEADERS ARRIVE

Then came the American settlers, and with the advent of these invincible frontiersmen a new era dawned. Texas history was truly in the making, and in a single generation the benefits derived from the privations and ceaseless constructive activities of the American colonists were greater than resulted from the nearly three full centuries of Spanish administrations. From 1821 to 1834, colonists from the United States settled in southeast Texas. Stephen F. Austin, "the Empresario" and "Father of Texas," was the first and most important colonizer. His colonies covered the lower Brazos and Colorado river basins including the site where the city of Austin now stands.

In 1830 the Mexican congress prohibited immigration from the United States. In 1833 Texans applied to Santa Anna for a separate government. The petition was denied. Stephen F. Austin was then sent to Mexico City to seek a repeal of the 1830 Mexican law prohibiting further immigration from the United States and to endeavor to get other difficulties between the Mexicans and the Texans settled so that Texas could be made a separate state. Upon his arrival in Mexico City, he was first given assurance that these two requests of the Texans would be granted. However, after waiting for a lengthy period for the requests to be officially granted, he wrote a letter to his comrades in Texas to wait no longer, but to proceed to seek separate statehood. His letter fell into the hands of Mexican officials and he was imprisoned.

After he finally was permitted to return to Texas, a brief battle between the Texans and the Mexicans occurred at Gonzales on October 2, 1835, where the Texans had in their possession a small cannon that the Mexicans demanded.

On November 3, 1835, the Texans set up a provisional government with Henry Smith as governor.

THE SIEGE AND MASSACRE OF THE ALAMO

On December 4 of that year (1835), Colonel Ben Milam asked a group of weary Texans, "Who will go with me into San Antonio?" With a tremendous shout, three hundred volunteers stepped forward. In San Antonio, Milam's group and other Texans won a decisive battle against General Cos' men and the Mexican general surrendered, but was released when he promised that he and his men would return to Mexico. Most of the Texans also left for their homes, leaving only about eighty men in San Antonio. In this battle, the brave leader, Ben Milam, lost his life.

In the meanwhile, General Santa Anna, having defeated his opponents in Mexico, arrived in San Antonio with between six and eight hundred well-equipped men.

When the huge Mexican army was known to be on its way to San Antonio, James Bowie was ordered to get together as many men as possible and to proceed to the aid of the few Texans still in San Antonio. Colonel W. B. Travis also arrived with about 20 men to add to Bowie's 25. Captain Patton reported with 11 soldiers and David Crockett arrived with some 12 or 14 men. These late arrivals, added

CRADLE OF TEXAS FREEDOM
The Alamo, erected about 1754 in San Antonio
(courtesy Texas Historical Commission)

to the 80 of the original garrison, totaled 150 plus a few Mexicans loyal to the Texans under Colonel Seguin. Probably the total number in the Alamo when the battle began was less than 180.

When scouts reported the approach of the large Mexican army, Travis and his men took shelter in the Alamo Mission, and sent the following urgent appeal to Judge Andrew Ponton at Gonzales:

> The enemy in large force is in sight. We want men and provisions. Send them to us. We have one hundred and fifty men, and are determined to defend the Alamo to the last. Give us assistance.
>
> W. B. TRAVIS, Lt. Col., Commanding
>
> P.S. Send an express to San Felipe with news night and day.
>
> Travis

The Alamo was a mission on the outskirts of San Antonio and though the walls were thick, it was not built for a fortress. There were no parapets and the walls were rambling and hard to defend. Colonel Travis, however, did everything possible to fortify them and succeeded to a limited extent.

The first day of siege, February 23, 1836, the Mexican force's demand for the Texans to surrender was answered with a shot from the Texas garrison. On the second day, the fort was bombarded during the day and Travis sent out his now famous message to the people of Texas:

> Commandancy of the Alamo,
> Bexar, February 24, 1836.
>
> To the People of Texas and all Americans in the world—Fellow Citizens and Compatriots:
>
> I am besieged with a thousand or more of the Mexicans under Santa Anna. I have sustained a continual bombardment and cannonade for twenty-four hours and have not lost a man. The enemy has demanded a surrender at discretion, otherwise, the garrison are to be put to the sword, if the fort is taken. I have answered their demand with a cannon shot and our flag still waves proudly from the walls. I shall never surrender or retreat. Then I call upon you in the name of liberty, or patriotism and everything dear to the American character, to come to our aid with dispatch. The enemy is receiving reinforcements daily

and will no doubt increase to three or four thousand in four or five days. If this call is neglected, I am determined to sustain myself as long as possible and die like a soldier who never forgets what is due his own honor and that of his country.

Victory or Death.

William Barret Travis
Lt. Col. Comdt.

P.S. The Lord is on our side. When the enemy appeared in sight we had not three bushels of corn. We have since found in deserted houses 80 to 90 bushels and got into the walls 20 to 30 head of beeves.

Travis

For thirteen days the Mexicans poured shells into the besieged fort, but not until March 6 did they finally scale the fort's walls and butcher the few remaining Texans who had by their valiant efforts, against insurmountable odds, made glorious history as they gave their lives.

By their heroic defense the Texans had lost a battle, but the massacre of Goliad and the butchery at the Alamo so rallied the Texans that it made it possible for an aroused Texas later to win the war.

TEXAS—A NEW UTOPIA

Stephen F. Austin's offer of 4,600 acres of land to each head of a family inaugurated a trek that brought within a few years families and groups from practically all of the Southern as well as many other states. By boat from New Orleans, by wagon train across Louisiana and the Indian Territory, men inspired with ambition and the love of adventure flocked to this new Utopia of which Austin, and later other empresarios, with glowing words had been telling the world. As a result, in 1828 Austin's colony contained 3,000 new Texans. In five years, 1833, the new empire numbered about 20,000 Anglo-Americans; and after gaining her independence from Mexico, in 1836 this number had increased to a little more than 50,000.

Independence Hall, located at Washington-on-the-Brazos, where on March 1, 1836, delegates assembled to declare the independence of Texas

Nuestra Senora de la Purisima Concepcion de Acuna Mission, better known as Mission Concepcion, located on Mission Road in San Antonio (courtesy Texas Historical Commission)

VICTORY AT SAN JACINTO

The site of the Texan victory was the San Jacinto Battlegrounds on the outskirts of the present city of Houston. It took place on April 21, 1836—a day all Texans now observe as San Jacinto Day.

Here occurred the famous battle often referred to as one of the most historic and decisive in world history. This battle resulted in the birth of a new nation—the Republic of Texas—and brought fame to General Sam Houston, former governor of Tennessee who commanded the Texas army. (General Houston was later president of the Republic of Texas, governor of the State of Texas, and U.S. senator from Texas.)

The San Jacinto Battle, within a few short weeks, followed defeats of the Texans by the Mexicans at Goliad and the Alamo. And so during the short duration of the battle—which lasted less than twenty minutes—cries of "Remember the Alamo" and "Remember Goliad" by the Texans did much to aid in the stampede of Santa Anna's much larger Mexican army and gave the victory to the Texans. The victory not only established the Republic of Texas, but resulted in later adding to the United States approximately one-third of its land area at the time.

SEEKERS ONLY OF OPPORTUNITY—AND PEACE

Not like the American colonists, who were seeking liberty and fleeing oppression, the Texas pioneers were in quest of economic betterment and adventure. However, soon they were confronted with the need of protecting not only their liberty, but their very lives against a dictator far more relentless than George III. At first no thought of conflict with the Spanish authorities entered their minds, for the early policies of Spanish Mexico toward her Texas colonists had been extremely liberal. Large grants of land were made to them, and no taxes or duties were imposed. The relationship between the Anglo-Americans and the Mexican government was cordial in the beginning. But following a series of revolutions begun in 1829, unscrupulous rulers successively seized power in Mexico. It was the unjust acts and despotic decrees of the new dictator, Santa Anna, which finally led to the Revolution of 1835-36 and the demand for independence.

The capture of Santa Anna at San Jacinto (courtesy Archives Division, Texas State Library)

In the Battle of San Jacinto were 910 Texans and approximately 1,600 Mexicans. The Mexicans lost 630 by death; 208 were wounded and 730 were captured. Nine Texans were killed or mortally wounded and 30 less seriously injured. Generals Santa Anna and Cos were taken prisoners; a general and other high officers were slain; a vast amount of property was taken including approximately 1,500 standards of arms, many swords, one nine-pound cannon, and $12,000 in silver.

WHEN THE TEXAS REPUBLIC BECAME THE TWENTY-EIGHTH STATE

For six weeks, Texas was legally the twenty-eighth state in the United States but was operated under the laws and officials of the Republic of Texas.

In a joint resolution, the Senate of the United States had accepted the offer of the Republic of Texas to join the Union, and on December 29, 1845, President James K. Polk signed the bill. This action, according to the view of United States officials, made Texas a state officially and a decree of the U.S. Supreme Court had so declared.

However, there was no telegraph, radio, or television available to carry news in those days and transportation was extremely slow. In addition, after the delayed news of the signing of the bill by President Polk was received by the Texas government, the change from the

---

HISTORICALLY TEXAS IS 470 YEARS OLD

It can be said that Texas is historically nearly five hundred years old. Actually its history dates from Captain Alonzo de Pineda's visit to the Texas coast and the map which he made at that time.

However, Texas probably had some inhabitants as long as 10,000 years ago. Whether these people of many centuries ago were Indians, or whether they were of some other race, we do not know. There is proof, though, that human life did exist here tens of thousands of years ago.

The reading of the Texas Declaraion of Independence, from the painting by Fanny V. and Charles B. Normann in the San Jacinto Museum of History (courtesy of Mr. Joe Fultz of Anderson, Texas, owner of the copyright)

25

Sam Houston's Executive Mansion in Washington, Texas (courtesy Archives Division, Texas State Library)

existing republican form of government to that of a state took time. An election had to be held to secure the legal officials, a new state government had to be organized, and the newly selected legislature had to be convened.

Consequently, it was mid-February 1846 before Texas was ready to operate as a state, and it was not until February 19 of that historic year that the Lone Star Flag was supplanted by the Stars and Stripes.

Even President Polk later realized the Texans were right in not changing their government until the proper arrangements to conduct it had been completed. He delayed appointing federal officers who would serve in Texas. He realized that a blunder had been made by the United States and he tried to correct it.

The first capitol of the Republic of Texas, located at Columbia, 1836-37

Therefore, the laws and officers of the Republic of Texas remained supreme in Texas until February 19, 1846. This decision had the approval of the officials of both the United States and the Republic of Texas.

TEN YEARS A REPUBLIC

Texas was a republic from April 21, 1836, until February 19, 1846, and then the red, white, and blue flag of the Republic of Texas, with its single star, was lowered for the last time and the Union's flag with twenty-eight stars was unfurled.

In 1861, Texas became the seventh state to join the Confederacy and soon all of the Southern states had seceded from the Union to form the Confederate States of America.

The Civil War ended in 1865, and Texas again took its place as a state of the United States.

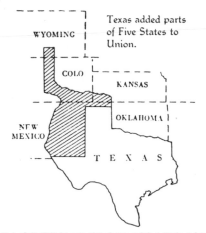

AREA OF TEXAS FROM 1836 TO 1850

As a result of the Texas victory over Mexico at San Jacinto on April 21, 1836, the Republic of Texas covered the area shown above.

In 1850, Texas sold the shaded section—parts of New Mexico, Oklahoma, Kansas, Colorado, and Wyoming—to the United States in order to pay its debts and to obtain funds necessary to conduct its government.

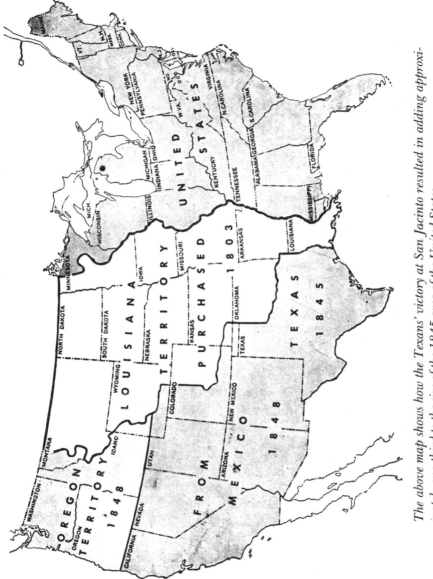

The above map shows how the Texans' victory at San Jacinto resulted in adding approximately one-third to the size of the 1845 area of the United States.

INFORMATION SOURCES

The material in this book is the fruit of many years' research by the author and his close association with such noted Texans as W. P. Zuber, one of the last survivors of the Battle of San Jacinto, L. W. Kemp, Texas historian, and others.

A few of the printed resources are:

History of Texas by Dr. Eugene C. Barker, The Southwest Press, 1929

A History of Texas for Schools by Mrs. Anna Hardwicke Pennybacker, 1908

Papers of Stephen F. Austin, edited by Eugene C. Barker, Government Printing, Washington, 1924

Romantic Flags of Texas by Mrs. Mamie Wynne Cox, Banks, Upshaw & Co., 1936

The Life of Stephen F. Austin by Eugene C. Barker, Cokesburg Press, 1925

Battle of San Jacinto by L. W. Kemp and Ed Kilman, 1947

Texas Heritage (series) by A. Garland Adair of Austin, Texas

THE TEXAS FLAGS

Indian Flag

It is well known that before the coming of the white man to Texas, numerous tribes of Indians were its only inhabitants. Where these red men came from, or how long they had been here before the arrival of the Spanish explorers, is a question upon which historians differ. Some—probably the majority—believe they were Asiatics (probably Mongolians) who came either from Eastern Asia across Bering Strait, which possibly had once been land joining Asia and America, or originated on this continent and some of them drifted into Asia later. The theory that they were originally Mongolians is strengthened by the fact that the early Indians were not really red men, but yellow men whose life in the open, plus scant clothing, had darkened their skins so that in reality they became men of bronze. Other historians believe they were descended from prehistoric tribes who originated on this continent.

The tribes which history places in and around the Houston area were primarily of the Caddoan family of Indians. This tribe, which contained many smaller groups, known in South and East Texas as the Caddos, the Orcoquisacas, and probably the Karankawas, were in the main friendly. Of these tribes, the Caddos and Orcoquisacas were inclined to be more settled and peaceful than the Karankawas. They generally remained in one locality and were even known to raise small crops, although they obtained most of their food from the abundance of wildlife and the streams and bayous nearby.

History records that various Indian tribes carried blood-red flags as they wandered up and down the coastal areas of Texas. Indian flags were generally made from buffalo hides, colored with paints made from herbs. The Indians often developed gruesome designs on their flags and were fond of unusual patterns.

The artist's conception of a flag of the first known Indians of Texas

Early Spanish Flag

History records the Spanish explorer Alonzo Alvarez de Pineda as the first white man to visit the land which is now Texas.

At dawn on a summer morning in the year 1519, more than a century before the Pilgrims set foot on American soil, this ancient explorer brought the first European flag to this part of the Western Hemisphere. The expedition came from the West Indies where, only twenty-seven years before, Columbus had landed when he discovered America. Pineda saw little of Texas, however, but did visit Galveston or possibly Matagorda Island.

History does not record a description of the flag or banner Pineda's party carried, nor are historians certain he had either, but ten years later a Spanish flag was unfurled here by Alvar Nunez Cabeza de Vaca. He and the survivors of the Panfilo de Narvaez expedition actually lived in Texas for several years. Notes and maps he had made while in Texas were published in 1542 and are regarded as the first contribution to Texas history.

The Spanish established the first permanent settlement of Europeans in Texas and were the first to give this area a territorial government.

However, they were slow in colonizing the vast area that is now Texas. From the latter part of the seventeenth century to the end of the eighteenth, Spain established thirty-nine missions, widely scattered throughout the area. But it was not until 1690 that the first Spanish settlement was made in East Texas. In 1821, with the Mexican victory over the Spanish, the reign of the Spanish over the land which is now Texas ended.

The earliest recorded Spanish flag was a church banner carrying the official seal of King Charles II. The one more often displayed in Texas was decorated with castles and lions. Known as the flag of Castile and Leon, it is the one most frequently pictured as the first of the Six Flags of Texas.

The early Spanish flag of Castile and Leon

Early French Flag

Following the Spanish early explorers and the establishments of many Spanish missions, René Robert Cavelier Sieur de La Salle brought the French to the coastal area of Texas a century later—1685. Historians differ as to which of the many colorful flags of King Louis XIV the expedition carried. However, as the golden lilies emblems of France were even then in popular favor, it may have been that flag with its pure white background, sprinkled with the gold (or yellow) fleurs-de-lis as shown here. Either by mistake or by intent, La Salle anchored his fleet off the shores of Texas, near Aransas Pass, in December 1684. Then following the coast eastward, and then up Lavaca Bay, they planted the flag of France at a site on the west bank of the Garcitas River, which La Salle then named Fort St. Louis. The party then continued northeast not far from the Gulf Coast—until one of his men brought the French explorer to his death with a bullet in his back.

The assassin's bullet, which killed La Salle near Navasota, Texas, on his third expedition, prevented him from fulfilling Louis XIV's plan for colonizing the area from the Mississippi to Mexico.

Nevertheless, La Salle's occupancy of Fort St. Louis on the Texas coast, while of short duration, probably resulted in the Anglo-American colonization of Texas more than a century earlier than it might have been, for it so alarmed the Spanish that they began a hurried occupation and settlement of the land they knew as Tejas.

In 1930 the Daughters of the American Revolution sponsored a suggestion by its state regent, and erected a bronze statue of René Robert Cavelier Sieur de La Salle at Navasota, the town nearest the spot where this noted French explorer was murdered by one of his own men.

An early French flag

Flag of the Republican Army
of the North

The second effort to capture Texas was made in 1812 by a former U.S. Army lieutenant, Augustus W. Magee, aided by Colonel Bernardo Gutierrez.

Magee and Gutierrez, accompanied by a volunteer army called the "Republican Army of the North," crossed the Sabine from the neutral ground and routed the Spanish at Nacogdoches.

In 1813, with a greatly augmented force, they successfully took over most of the territory east of San Antonio. On April 2, with an army grown to more than seven hundred, they defeated the Spanish at San Antonio and set up a republican government with Gutierrez as governor. However, after about six months, many Americans became dissatisfied with the cruelty shown the prisoners and deserted, and the Spanish then brought forth a large army of more than four thousand men and recaptured San Antonio. Later, on August 18, the Republican Army of the North, badly disorganized, was disbanded. Gutierrez, at this time, had returned to the United States and Magee had died.

During their successful march, halfway across Texas and later at their victory at San Antonio, the Magee army flew an emerald flag. Some historians maintain that, because of Magee's temporary control of San Antonio and most of the eastern area which is now the State of Texas, Texans had lived not under six flags but under seven.

The success of the Republican Army of the North—even though of short duration—gave many adventurers of the United States dreams of the conquest of the land of the Tejas. Following the defeat of the British at New Orleans, many sought a new life in the land beyond the Sabine.

Because of its limited existence, no foreign government gave recognition to the Magee-Gutierrez administration and few historians include its banner as one of the sovereign flags under which early Texas was governed.

Flag of the Republican Army of the North

Don Louis de Aury's Flag

In 1815 Don Louis de Aury, a naval officer who had been involved in revolutions in Granada, La Plata, Venezuela, and Mexico and who later became a buccaneer of note, accepted a commission from the Mexico revolutionists to establish a post for the Mexicans at Galveston. After the first revolution of the Mexicans against the Spanish was defeated, de Aury set up his own domain on Galveston Island. Here he began a systematic piracy of any vessel that could be seized. The flag which flew from the masts of his three heavily armed vessels had a white field with a wide red border, and in the center was painted a green wreath with a sword and an olive branch in blue.

In 1816 de Aury was joined by Captain Henry Perry, formerly an officer who had been with Magee's expedition—the Republican Army of the North. Xavier Mina, another of these officers, had brought three ships to Galveston Island from Spain. The three men agreed to invade Mexico from the coast. Failure finally became their lot. Mina was killed, Perry took his own life, and later in the year de Aury left Galveston and lived for about a year in Central America.

De Aury and his associates probably did more harm than good during their lives on Galveston Island, but their actions did much to encourage the Americans who were interested in making Texas a new frontier for the Anglo-Americans.

Because for a short period the Republican Army of the North had complete control of most of Texas and for nearly a year controlled the area with a full roster of governmental officials, de Aury had hoped to succeed where the Republican Army of the North had failed—to conquer the Texas area for Anglo-Americans.

Don Louis de Aury's flag

Lafitte's Venezuelan Flag

In 1817, de Aury decided that piracy paid better than revolutions, and he returned to Galveston only to find that the famous pirate, Jean Lafitte, had taken over the island.

Lafitte remained in complete possession of Galveston Island from 1818 to 1821, when Lieutenant Kearney, commander of the USS *Enterprise*, forced him to leave because it had been reported that Lafitte, or his men, had fired on American vessels. Lafitte always claimed that he was an honest man and preyed only upon Spanish ships. He did render great aid to General Jackson in 1815 at the Battle of New Orleans and always strongly denied he had ever attacked American vessels. He was said to have hanged two of his lieutenants for attacking American vessels.

Lafitte lived pretentiously, like an emperor in a palace he called Maison Rouge. His village was known as Campeachy. At the masthead of his ships he first had a simple red flag, but later, and for a longer period, he flew the Venezuelan flag—yellow, blue, and red striped, with the yellow on top and the red at the bottom. The same flag was at one time used by de Aury.

Lafitte flew the Venezuelan flag with the consent of that country and was said to have been commissioned to prey upon Spanish ships by that government.

After the United States forced Lafitte off Galveston Island, he lived in splendor in Mexico. This most daring and colorful of the Texas filibusters died in Yucatan in 1826.

Venezuelan flag carried by Lafitte

Colonel Long's Flag

Doctor (Colonel) James Long was one of the best educated and most cultured of the Texas filibuster leaders.

While serving as a surgeon in the U.S. Army at New Orleans, he dreamed of Americanizing the province of Texas, and as time passed he resolved to make this dream come true.

Dr. Long met and married the beautiful and cultured niece of General James Wilkinson who financed his effort to take Texas from the Spanish. It is said that Dr. Long also had the blessing of General Andrew Jackson, the hero of the famous victory over the British at New Orleans in 1815.

In 1819, Dr. Long, then under his title of colonel, with a large number of men set up a government at Nacogdoches and declared Texas a republic.

Success was short-lived, and Colonel Long and his wife returned to Louisiana for safety. However, in 1821, the Longs, accompanied by a few recruits, reached Galveston. From there, Long planned to capture Goliad. They were successful at first, but shortly were captured by a sizeable army under a Mexican revolution command. Long was taken to Mexico City, where he was later shot by a Mexican soldier under mysterious circumstances—without the sanction of the Mexican government. The life of Mrs. Long, especially after Long's capture, is another interesting chapter in Texas history, and every Texan should read it in full. She often has been referred to as the "Mother of Texas."

Colonel Long's flag was of red and white stripes, much like our national flag, but it centered in its union a single white star—the first of the Texas flags with a Lone Star.

Colonel Long's flag of 1817

Mexico's Historic Flag

For the better part of eleven years—from 1810 to 1821—Mexico struggled to free herself from the iron hand of the Spanish dictators who had ruled Mexico since the conquest by Cortes.

Finally, on September 27, 1821, Mexican independence was achieved, and on October 24, 1824, the name "the United States of Mexico" was adopted. In 1825 the Republic of Mexico's flag—three vertical bars of equal width—was officially designated. At the flag's staff is a bar of green, the center stripe is of white, and the other is red. An eagle grasping a snake in its mouth occupies the better part of the white, or center, stripe. This flag, from 1825 up to the Texas victory at San Jacinto, waved over most of Texas, and was even carried into Texas by Mexican troops as late as 1842. It remains—with a few minor changes—the official flag of Mexico today.

Most of the citizens of Texas sympathized with the Mexicans in their quest for liberty from the Spanish, and Texans and the new Mexican government were on friendly terms. Even when Santa Anna began his invasion of Texas, Anglo-American opposition was directed against Santa Anna, rather than the Mexican people.

Today the United States and Mexico are close and cordial neighbors and now work with their ally to the north, Canada, in unison for the maintenance and welfare of the North American continent.

Mexico's historic flag

The Flag of Texas Conservatives

The flag in general use in Texas during the campaign against the Mexicans, especially by that faction of Texans who were known as the Conservatives, was the flag of 1824. This flag was favored by many Texans who wanted to show their desire to make peace with the Mexican officials. In fact, probably a majority of the Texans of that period looked upon it as Texas's official flag in 1835 and 1836.

The Conservatives were ever hopeful that affairs between the Anglo-Americans living in Texas and the Mexican government could be settled without a war. Therefore, in order not to offend the Mexicans unnecessarily, they adopted the green, white, and red flag of Mexico, minus the eagle which was on the official Mexican flag. In place of the eagle, the Texans inserted the figures "1824," which announced to the world that they were for Mexico only if the Constitution of 1824 were observed. The Mexican Constitution of 1824 offered relief to the Anglo-Americans who were at that time being oppressed by the Mexican government of that period.

Many believe this flag was among those in the Alamo when it fell. Both McArdle and Gentily, noted artists who have painted many pictures of Texas early days, display this flag in their paintings.

This flag was also credited with having been the official flag of the Texans when they defeated General Cos at the Siege of San Antonio in December of 1835. It was also recorded as often being flown at the masts of several ships of the First Navy of Texas.

48

Flag of Texas Conservatives, 1835-36

Fredonian Rebellion Flag

While it was of short duration, and had little immediate effect on any but those living in extreme East Texas, Hayden Edwards' rebellion against the Mexican authorities in 1826 became an important reason for the distrust that the Mexicans began to display of all Anglo-Americans. For this reason, the Fredonian Rebellion, while unsuccessful, was a major factor in creating strained relations between the Mexicans and the colonists, and after ten years of strife finally resulted in the Texas Revolution.

Edwards had been conveyed a large grant of land in East Texas by the Mexican government and was authorized to settle 800 families there. However, he endeavored to force those who were there earlier to move or pay him for their land. As many of these were Mexicans, this caused the Mexican government to cancel his grant and order him to leave Texas.

Angered because he had vested much of his fortune in his new venture, Edwards refused to abide by these demands. Together with a few loyal friends and the aid of the Cherokee Indians in the area, he organized a small army, declared Texas independent of Mexico, and gave battle under the name "the Republic of Fredonia."

Edwards endeavored to get assistance from Austin's colonists, but they decided not to join the rebellion. Soon the Indians withdrew their aid, and realizing that his little army was deserting the cause, he gave up his fight and returned to the United States.

Edwards' flag of white and red with the inscription "Independence, Freedom and Justice" was displayed years later in the little town of Clinton in Harris County at a meeting of citizens. It was received warmly, for Edwards had many friends in Texas.

Fredonian Rebellion flag

Old Come and Take It

An early Texas flag with a most visible warning to the Mexicans who were threatening a Texan garrison in 1835 at Gonzales was "Old Come and Take It." On its white silk field—painted in black—was a five-pointed star, a cannon barrel, and the famous words, "Come and Take It."

Its creation resulted from a demand of the Mexicans on the Texans who had gathered at Gonzales under Colonel John H. Moore to give up a cannon the Texans had borrowed from the Mexican garrison at San Antonio. The cannon was lent to the Texans in order to help them defend Gonzales from Indian attacks.

Early in October of 1835, the Texans' reply to the demand was a shot from the little cannon which, for the time, sent the Mexicans on their way, without the loss of a single Texan. One Mexican was killed and several were wounded.

This, the first battle of the Texas-Mexican War excepting minor skirmishes at Anahuac and Velasco, was known as the "Lexington of the Texas Revolution."

The famous flag was said to have been made of silk cut from the wedding gown of Naomi De Witt, a daughter of Green De Witt, noted Texas empresario.

The Gonzales flag was not in as many battles as some of the others, but it was, and is, one of the best known flags of the Texas Revolution. It is a revered symbol of the brave men of that time, and dear to all Texans. In addition to being the first battle flag of the Texas Revolution, it was also the first Texas banner unfurled in a successful battle against the Mexicans.

The Gonzales banner of 1835, "Old Come and Take It"

Scott's Flag of the Liberals

During the year before the Texans won their great victory at San Jacinto, the inhabitants of the area were divided into two factions—the Conservatives and the Liberals. The Mexican flag of 1824 was the one the Conservatives rallied behind, for they still hoped for a just settlement with Mexico.

The Liberals, however, had given up all hope for any solution to their differences with the Mexican government, and wanted a complete break with Santa Anna and his leaders. In the fall of 1835, Captain William Scott, a wealthy Kentuckian who formed a company at his home near Lynchburg, designed a flag around which the Liberals rallied. This flag was carried at the Battle of Concepcion by James McGahey. The Battle of Concepcion, one of the first real battles of the Texas Revolution, occurred October 28, 1835, just a few weeks after the Battle of Gonzales. About ninety men under James W. Fannin and James Bowie, surrounded by a Mexican force of nearly four hundred, won a victory over the enemy.

According to historians, when McGahey was wounded he gave the flag to one of Fannin's men, Thomas Bell, who carried it in the Siege of San Antonio, December 6, 1835. Of blue silk, with a large white star in the center, the flag had in large letters at the bottom the word "Independence."

The Conservatives were opposed to the use of the word "Independence" on the flag as they still believed that peace with the Mexicans might be secured without open conflict. However, the Liberals held to their flag during much of the Texas Revolution.

Scott's flag of the Liberals

Siege of San Antonio Flag

When the daring Captain William Brown took part in the success-ful Siege of San Antonio in December 1835, historians say that his "Bloody Flag" was flying at the head of his company.

This flag, perhaps the most famous one of an arresting design, had thirteen stripes of alternate red and white with a union of blue. Outlined across its union was a man's huge, sinewy arm holding a bloody sword. On one of the stripes was the word "Independence." It was a banner that struck terror into the hearts of the enemy, and which left no doubt that this company of Texans meant to fight for liberty. The group which fought under this flag was one of the most active of the Texas army, as well as one of the most successful.

After the storming of San Antonio, Captain Brown carried his flag to Velasco, and there on January 8, 1836, it was run to topmast in front of the American Hotel.

Historian John Henry Brown states that Captain Brown's flag and a Lone Star Flag were hoisted over the building where the Convention met when it declared for independence.

Captain Brown and his brother, Jeremiah, became famous as officers of the Texas Navy after the victory at San Jacinto. In a letter from President David G. Burnet to Major James Collinsworth, April 12, 1836, the president advised: "A prize (the Brig Pocket) of considerate value, was brought into Galveston a few days ago by Captain J. Brown."

Brown's flag

Captain Baker's San Felipe Flag

In 1834, Captain Moseley Baker of Alabama came to Texas and, being thoroughly in harmony with the ideals and spirit of the Texans, joined the company of young men raised by William Barret Travis.

This group of volunteers, of which Baker was the captain, saw service in several engagements in the southern part of Texas. Many early Texans claimed that the San Felipe flag, show on the opposite page, was borne by General Sidney Sherman's regiment on that victorious April 21, 1836, when, at San Jacinto, Texas won its independence from Mexico.

This historical flag embodied in its colorful folds parts of the flags of three nations, and of a coveted wilderness which brave men were endeavoring to make into a new republic.

The upper union contained a blue field with red bars to represent the British Jack of that period. The thirteen stripes—alternating red and white—were symbolic of the Stars and Stripes of the United States; on the white bars were the words, "Our Country's Rights or Death." The lower union of green was to remind all who viewed it that they intended to set up this Mexican state as a free republic. Last, but most important to those daring men of yesterday, was the white star—the five-pointed star—which set Texas apart as the one state in the Mexican Confederation which intended to fight for its freedom.

This flag was presented to the company by Gail Borden, Jr., on March 2, 1836. Captain Baker's flag was given the name of San Felipe in honor of the capital of Stephen F. Austin's colony. So much did it resemble the flag proposed by Stephen F. Austin for the republic that it may have been designed on the basis of a letter from Austin to Borden, describing his design.

Captain Moseley Baker's flag

Sarah Dodson's Lone Star Flag

Sarah Rudolph Bradley Dodson, a native of Kentucky, in September 1835 designed a flag for a company of Harrisburg volunteers ready to depart for action against the Mexicans. This flag, the first tricolor Lone Star Flag ever to fly in the Texas air, was more like the present flag than any of the others that led brave men in battle against their oppressors.

It was composed of three equal vertical bars. The first one near the staff was of blue and contained a large white five-pointed star in its center; the second, or center bar, was of white; and the third was of red.

Mrs. Dodson, who was Sarah Rudolph Bradley before her marriage to Archelaus B. Dodson on May 17, 1835, was a bride of only a few months when her husband marched away with the Harrisburg Company of Volunteers to aid in freeing Texas. She at once set to work designing the colorful flag that history now knows as the Sarah Dodson Flag.

In the hands of James Ferguson of the Harrisburg Volunteers, the flag was first displayed at Gonzales and later unfurled during the Siege of San Antonio on December 6, 1835.

Brown's *History of Texas* states that the Dodson flag was also flown from a staff atop the building where the Convention declared Texas independent.

The claim has been made that it was the Troutman flag of the Georgia troops which was at Washington in March 1836, instead of the Dodson flag. The Troutman flag could not have been at Washington-on-the-Brazos for the wind caught it in its ropes at Goliad on March 8 and it was so badly torn that it was discarded.

*The first tricolor Lone Star Flag of Texas,
designed by Sarah Dodson of Kentucky*

Flag over the Alamo

New Orleans furnished two companies of volunteers in the fight for Texas independence, and the members of these two groups of enthusiastic young men were known as the "New Orleans Grays."

They were first organized in November 1835, and reached San Antonio in time to help drive the Mexicans from the city. This Texas victory occurred three months before the fall of the Alamo, where many of one group of the New Orleans volunteers gave their lives. Many members of the other company were massacred at Goliad on Palm Sunday, March 27, 1836. When one company of the Grays arrived in Texas, large, enthusiastic crowds greeted its members and cannons roared a welcome.

The flag of the New Orleans Grays was of bright blue silk on which appeared the inscription: "First Company of Texan Volunteers, from New Orleans." An eagle carried in its beak a streamer on which appeared the words: "God & Liberty."

Historians have not been united on which flags flew over the ramparts of Fort Alamo but, because the Mexicans claim they tore down the flag of the New Orleans volunteers and put up the Mexican flag, the Grays' banner was probably one of them.

The activities of these patriotic New Orleans volunteers, who so valiantly aided the Texas cause, is recorded in a diary kept by one of its members. It has been preserved by the University of Texas and is now in the archives of the university.

Many maintain that the Mexican flag of 1824 also flew atop the Alamo, and a book written partly by him quotes Davy Crockett as saying, "We have had a large national flag made. It is composed of thirteen stripes, red and white alternating, with a large white star of five points in the center and between the points the letters T-E-X-A-S."

Flag over the Alamo, March 6, 1836

Alabama Red Rovers Flag

The Red Rovers was a company of Alabamians who came to Texas in the fall of 1835. Most of the Red Rovers were massacred with Fannin at Goliad, shortly after their first and last fight. A few of them escaped the massacre and lived to relate the details of the treachery of the Mexicans.

The Mexicans broke faith with the Alabamians who had agreed to surrender under the regular rules of war, marched them to Goliad, and massacred them on Palm Sunday, March 27, 1836.

The Red Rovers carried a plain red flag and even their uniforms were of red. They made a colorful picture as they arrived in January of 1836 to bolster the Texan forces.

According to R. L. Dickson, a grandson of Abishai Dickson who was one of the Red Rovers killed at Goliad, the Red Rovers flag is now in a Mexico City museum, having been captured during the massacre at Goliad.

Dr. (Captain) John Schackleford of Courtland, Alabama, who sympathized with the Texas cause and had followed Texas events closely, provided the arms and necessary equipment for seventy-five men and recruited the company. In the massacre of Fannin's men at Goliad, Captain Schackleford's life was spared. He was retained by the Mexicans as a surgeon and managed to save the lives of many of the wounded Mexicans. Eventually he escaped and returned to his home in Courtland, Alabama.

The Alabama Red Rovers flag

Johanna Troutman's Goliad Flag

One of the famous first flags of the Texas Republic was made by Johanna Troutman, often called the Betsy Ross of Texas. Miss Troutman was born in Knoxville, Georgia, in 1817. She was the daughter of Colonel C. A. Troutman of that Georgia city. In 1835, hearing an appeal from Colonel Fannin for a Georgia battalion to aid the Texas cause, she did much to bring success to the effort of Captain William Ward and others to raise the battalion which came to Texas in December 1835. Before the volunteers left for Texas, she designed, completed, and presented to them a flag of white silk, bearing a blue, five-pointed star and the inscription, "Liberty or Death." One historian relates that on the other side was printed in large letters, "Where Liberty Dwells, There Is My Home." The flag, first unfurled at Velasco on January 8, 1836, above the American Hotel, was carried to Goliad by Colonel Fannin, who raised it as the national flag of the Republic of Texas.

During the Goliad campaign, the flag caught in the ropes which had been used to hoist it, and in the hurry to get it down, it was completely destroyed.

Miss Troutman is buried in the State Cemetery at Austin and the state has erected a life-size monument of gray granite over her grave. In the State Capitol is a painting of this beautiful young girl who did so much to inspire the early Texans to victory.

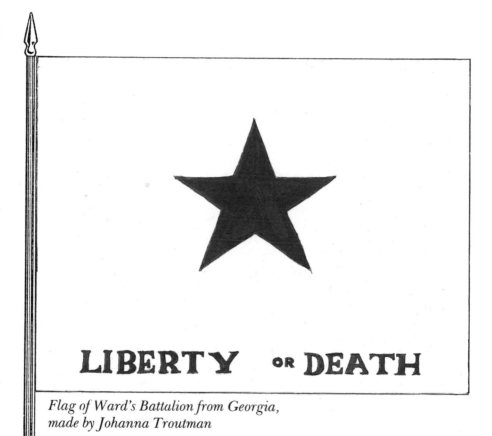

Flag of Ward's Battalion from Georgia,
made by Johanna Troutman

Red Flag of San Fernando Mission

Much to the displeasure of the holy priests of San Fernando Mission in San Antonio, Mexico's dictator, Santa Anna, once used the mission for a signal tower.

In February 1836, just prior to the fall of the Alamo, Santa Anna had a blood-red flag hoisted to the top of the highest tower of San Fernando Mission, proclaiming to the Texans that for them there would be no quarter.

Before raising his red flag, Santa Anna sent a messenger to the Texans demanding their unconditional surrender. The Texans received the messenger courteously, but answered Santa Anna's demand with a cannon shot aimed at the Mexicans, and the Mexican general then unfurled his blood-red flag over the mission.

Travis, hero of the Alamo, in his last published letter said: "A blood-red banner waves from the Church of Bexar [San Fernando Mission] and in the camp above us, in token that the war is one of vengeance against rebels, they have declared as such."

A story of the Battle of San Jacinto often related by descendants of that notable battle tells of how just before the Texans began their charge, a soldier drew a red bandanna handkerchief from his pocket, tied it to a long stick, raised it aloft, and amid mighty roars from the throats of all near, a blood-red flag floated on San Jacinto Battlefield. And the Texans surged solidly forward shouting, "Remember the Alamo! Remember Goliad!"

That red bandanna, raised aloft and waving in the air, inspired the Texans to greater strength and enthusiasm, and no quarter was given Santa Anna that afternoon.

The Texans had had their revenge.

The red flag of San Fernando Mission

San Jacinto Flag

The flag which won the greatest glory of all during the Texas campaign, and in addition created one of the often quoted love stories of all time, was the San Jacinto Flag. A gift of the ladies of Newport, Kentucky, it was presented to General Sidney Sherman, whose regiment of Texas infantry bore it so heroically in the Battle of San Jacinto. Made of white silk and fringed with gold, or yellow, braid, it contained the figure of a woman holding in her hand a sword and on the sword was a banner with the words, "Liberty or Death."

Before leaving for Texas, James A. Sylvester, one of the Kentuckians who was with Sherman at San Jacinto, asked his beautiful dancing partner for something as a souvenir. She drew a long red glove from her arm and gave it to him. Sylvester carried the glove at the top of his flagstaff wherever he went, but in the Battle of San Jacinto, it was lost and never found. Sylvester was one of the three Texans who captured Santa Anna.

On the afternoon of April 21, 1836, as the drums beat a tattoo, the flute of Frederick Limski of Captain Andrew Briscoe's Company loudly played "Will You Come to the Bower." Instantly the cries of "Remember the Alamo! Remember Goliad!" pierced the woods of San Jacinto. The San Jacinto Flag, held high by Private Sylvester, led the Texans forward and to victory.

Many years later this famous old flag, after being restored to its original appearance, was presented to the State of Texas. It was given to the state by the descendants of General Sidney Sherman. It is now on view in a glass case behind the Speaker's desk in the House of Representatives at Austin.

The San Jacinto Flag, Kentucky's gift to Texas

Texas Naval Flag of 1836

Historians have rarely recorded the true importance of the Texas Navy in the winning of the Texas Revolution against the Mexican dictator. But without the efficient and effective work of the Texas Navy in preventing the landing of Mexican troops and supplies at Texas coastal cities during the campaign, the victory would probably have not been won, or at least would have been greatly postponed.

On April 9, 1836, President David G. Burnet authorized the flag designed by Commodore Hawkins as the Texas Naval Flag. Its field of thirteen alternate red and white stripes was a reproduction of the flag of the United States except that its union of blue bore only one large, white five-pointed star in the center. Its similarity to the United States flag often confused the Mexican warships and when they saw it waving in the breeze, they hurried away without giving battle.

The first of these flags was made by the ladies of Harrisburg. As cloth was not plentiful in those days, it is said that one of the ladies ripped up her red flannel petticoat, which was used to supply material for the seven red stripes of the flag.

Later, the Second Texas Navy, under command of Commodore Edwin Moore, added glory to the history of the Navy of the Republic of Texas.

The Republic of Texas's official Naval Flag

First Flag of Texas

The first official flag of the Republic of Texas, designed by General Lorenzo de Zavala, was adopted by the Convention held at Washington-on-the-Brazos, May 11, 1836, shortly after the victory at San Jacinto.

This flag had a blue field with a white five-pointed star in its center. Around the star were the letters *T-E-X-A-S*.

The flag, according to minutes of the Convention, was officially selected, first by a committee of five of Texas first citizens, and then by the Convention, but there is no authentic written evidence that it was ever displayed.

It was, at least officially, the first flag adopted by the new republic, and was one of the most attractive of the many designed by early Texans.

The Third Congress of the Republic of Texas held in Houston, on January 21, 1839, officially adopted as the national flag of the new republic the present Lone Star Flag of Texas. President Mirabeau B. Lamar signed the resolution into law on January 25, 1839.

General de Zavala at one time was a citizen of Mexico and a member of its congress. Later he was private secretary to Santa Anna. He was a leading factor in the compiling of the Mexican Constitution of 1824 but joined the Texan forces when Santa Anna repudiated the Constitution. Because of his great aid to the Texas cause, he was made the first vice-president of the Republic of Texas.

*De Zavala's flag, once the official flag of
the Republic of Texas*

Captain Burroughs' Flag from Ohio

Ohio was one of the distant states which several times demonstrated its desire to aid the Texans' quest for liberty. First, the enthusiastic group of young men from Ohio and Kentucky who fought at San Jacinto under General Sidney Sherman departed for the Texas War from Cincinnati, and Ohio citizens contributed the famous "Twin Sisters" cannon which played such a conspicuous part in the defense against the Mexicans.

Then, when Captain George H. Burroughs and others from Ohio—joined by Captain Morgan's Company from Philadelphia— came to Texas, they united under the banner of one of the most artistic flags of the Texas Revolution. This flag, presented by the ladies of Zanesville, Ohio, had a field of light blue silk. Upon a deeper blue ground was a five-pointed star of yellow, with the letters *T-E-X-A-S* between the points. Above stood the American eagle, holding in its beak a streamer, gracefully encircling the star, upon which was inscribed, "Hero of San Jacinto." In the lower staff corner of the flag was printed, "Zanesville, Ohio."

Captain Burroughs and his men arrived too late to help Texas win its independence, but not too late to aid them in keeping it. The Mexicans were still invading Texas, regardless of Santa Anna's capture and his promises to the victors. From September of 1836 to August of 1837, the group served under General Felix Huston, who was then commander of the Texas army, and history records that they rendered valuable service to the Texas cause during this eventful period.

Captain Burroughs' flag from Ohio

President David Burnet's Flag

The First Congress of the Republic of Texas, meeting in Columbia in December 1836, thought it advisable to alter the design of the first official flag of Texas, adopted in May 1836.

David G. Burnet, the first president of the Republic of Texas, suggested that Texas's official flag be an azure blue with a single gold star in its center.

Gammell's *Laws of Texas* Volume 1, page 1132, quotes the resolution which was passed by this First Congress creating this flag. This resolution was enacted and signed by Ira Ingram, speaker of the House, and Richard Ellis, president pro tem of the Senate, and is dated December 10, 1836. It also carried the signature of the president, Sam Houston.

While it was the official Texas flag until 1839 when the Texas flag of today was adopted, it was seldom referred to and no record of where or when it was displayed has been noted. This flag, adopted several months after the de Zavala flag, was probably adopted as a simplification of the de Zavala standard. The two flags were much alike. However, the Burnet flag's huge five-pointed star was of gold, or yellow, instead of white and the lettering *T-E-X-A-S* was omitted.

The young Texas Republic was governed, in its early period, by patriotic men, but men who had had little experience in government. Consequently, they often had a change of mind and ideas. This accounts for the official designation of both de Zavala's and Burnet's flags, and the fact that neither was ever known to be publicly displayed.

Burnet's flag, the second official flag of the Republic of Texas

Lone Star Flag

The beautiful, inspiring flag that waves over Texas today was created and officially dedicated only after a score of other flags had first been the banners under which Texans so valiantly fought for freedom.

Santa Anna once scornfully said, "The Texans flatter themselves they have a government, and are fighting under no recognized flag." At that time, Texas had many flags under which brave and determined Texans soon conquered this self-styled Napoleon of the West, and within just a few months it had a government which has endured for five generations.

Texas soon had a permanent official flag—the Lone Star Flag—designed by Dr. Charles B. Stewart, second signer of the Texas Declaration of Independence and long a devoted Texas citizen and patriot. The Lone Star Flag was approved, first by a committee composed of six signers of the Texas Declaration of Independence, namely: Lorenzo de Zavala, William B. Scates, Thomas Barnett, Sterling C. Robertson, Thomas J. Gazley, and Richard Ellis. The red, white, and blue flag, with but a single star in its union of blue, was officially designated in 1839.

Governor E. M. Pease once said of Dr. Stewart, "He was never a seeker after public position, but he never shirked responsibilities placed upon him. He lived and died fond of his friends, loyal to his government and his country."

The original design of the flag is now in custody of a granddaughter, Mr. H. W. Fling, of Houston.

Texas's Lone Star Flag of today

United States Flag of 1846

Ever since June 14, 1777, the Stars and Stripes has been the inspiration of Americans, and its only change has been the adding and arrangement of the stars, made necessary by the continuous admission of new states.

The twenty-eighth of these stars was in honor of the new State of Texas, which first entered the Union more than one hundred years ago. Its star was officially placed upon the Star Spangled Banner in 1846. The United States Congress agreed to a joint resolution that joined Texas to the United States on December 28, 1845.

A dramatic scene was presented to the crowd assembled at the Texas Capitol on February 19, 1846, when, on order of President Anson Jones, the Lone Star Flag of Texas was slowly lowered from its lofty staff and in its place was hoisted the newly made Star-Spangled Banner, with its twenty-eight stars. As the new symbol of statehood for Texas gayly floated in the breeze, President Jones sadly said, "The final act in this drama is now performed. The Republic of Texas is no more."

It was an eventful day for the Lone Star State, one in which joy at the new association with the twenty-seven allied states was mingled with the sorrow that came with the ending of the life of the Republic of Texas. And in the assembly were hundreds who had served not only under the Lone Star Flag of the Republic but under other flags which inspired and encouraged the men whose bravery and privations were responsible for the establishment of the Texas Republic.

United States flag of 1846

The Stars and Bars

On secession, the Confederate States of America immediately established its own government and officially dedicated its first flag. The first national flag of the Confederacy had a blue union with a circle of seven stars on it and its field consisted of three stripes—red, white, and red.

Many flags were later created for the Confederacy, but the Stars and Bars, as originally made official, was the one most commonly displayed. For generations the designer of this flag has been in question. Many say the artist, Nicola Marschall, was the creator, while others believe Major Orren Randolph Smith designed it.

While additional Southern states soon joined the Confederacy, the Stars and Bars as originally designed, with its seven stars representing the first seven states to secede, remained in favor.

Officially, other stars were to be added as states joined the Confederacy, but so popular did the Stars and Bars become that it remained in use throughout the Civil War.

At the time the Stars and Bars was first displayed, Texas was the seventh state to join the Confederacy, being preceded by South Carolina, Mississippi, Florida, Alabama, Georgia, and Louisiana.

The daughter of President John Tyler of Virginia unfurled the first Stars and Bars.

The first official Confederate flag was raised over the capitol building in Montgomery, Alabama, on March 4, 1861.

*The Stars and Bars, the first national flag
of the Confederate States of America*

Confederate Battle Flag

Seen across the fields of battle, the Stars and Bars of the Confederacy and the Stars and Stripes of the Union were much alike. A tragic incident occurred at Manassas, when Southerners failed to distinguish the difference between the two flags and several Southerners lost their lives. It is of record that after the Battle of Manassas both North and South accused each other of carrying imitations of the other's flag. This caused confusion on both sides and resulted in the creation of the Battle Flag of the Confederacy.

This flag has a red field upon which a Saint Andrew's cross of blue, edged with white, extends diagonally from corner to corner. Seven five-pointed stars of equal size are imposed upon each strip of the blue cross, although only thirteen stars are visible.

The Battle Flag became a favorite of the Southern soldiers, and even today it is displayed often—especially in the South. The Battle Flag was square, and was made in several sizes. Exclusive of a wide white border used for tying to the staff, many were 30 × 30 inches, 36 × 36 inches, and some even 48 × 48 inches.

The Naval Jack of the Confederacy was of the same design as the Battle Flag, but elongated. Its length was one and one-half times its depth.

Another Confederate Jack had a blue field upon which seven white stars were placed in a circle.

A naval ensign of the Confederacy had two bars of red and one of white in the center and a blue union containing twelve white stars.

The Confederate Battle Flag

The Bonnie Blue Flag

Because historians give credit to the First Company of Texas Confederate Volunteers as the first to display it at the head of a Confederate marching column, the Bonnie Blue Flag is recognized as wholly Texan.

This beautiful and inspiring banner of blue silk, with a five-pointed star in its center, became one of the most beloved of the Confederate battle flags. When on dress parade, it often had a border of gold, or yellow, fringe.

At Richmond, when General Grant was storming that city, the Bonnie Blue Flag was much in evidence. Numerous other Confederate troops also carried it into many battles.

General Robert E. Lee is quoted as saying, "Give me more Texans and I will feel more sure of victory." Texans—and Southerners—never wavered when the Bonnie Blue Flag was unfurled.

The song "The Bonnie Blue Flag" was also sung in many Southern states and its words and music were a hit throughout the South during the Civil War.

The song was at its height of popularity in New Orleans when General Butler of the invading Union army took possession of the city. The general was so annoyed at the words and the tune that he issued orders forbidding a display of the flag or singing of the song. Below is the first stanza of "The Bonnie Blue Flag":

> We are a band of brothers, and native to the soil,
> Fighting for the property we gathered by honest toil;
> And when our rights were threatened, the cry arose near
> and far,
> Hurrah! for the Bonnie Blue Flag that bears a single
> star.

The Bonnie Blue Flag

Old Glory

To Americans, the most glorious and the most beautiful of all flags is Old Glory, this nation's official flag of today.

Old Glory had its birth at the time our people were struggling for liberty and for that democracy which Americans now cherish and hold so dear. It is one of the oldest flags in the world, having undergone no change since its adoption except the addition of stars which represent new states added to the Union. There are few nations which can boast that their flags have undergone no change in the past two hundred years. Americans also rejoice that their history for a century and a half has followed the general course begun when the Stars and Stripes first came into use.

Henry Ward Beecher, in referring to the adoption of the flag, said:

> In 1777, on the fourteenth of June, Congress of the Colonies assembled and ordained this glorious National Flag which we now hold and defend, and advance it full high before God and all men as the flag of Liberty. It was no holiday flag, gorgeously emblazoned for gaiety or vanity. It was a solemn signal. When that banner first unrolled to the sun it was the symbol of all those holy truths and purposes which brought together the Colonial American Congress.

Old Glory is a symbol, the sacred symbol of all that true Americans hold dear. Under its warm colors of red, white, and blue, millions have ever fought victoriously, and many thousands willingly have died so that all that its silken folds represent might be preserved.

As Beecher so aptly added to his tribute, "When understanding hearts see their national flag, they see not the flag, but the nation itself."

Old Glory

City of Houston Flag

Houston was named for General Sam Houston, whose army led Texas to its independence from Mexico in 1836. The city became the capital of the Republic of Texas from 1837 to 1839, and later grew with the oil business on the Gulf Coast.

On May 24, 1915, Houston's mayor declared to the City Council that the city needed to adopt a flag, and he asked that a committee be formed to choose the design. The resulting flag was adopted later that year.

The design that was selected is of a five-pointed star on a blue field. In a circle inside the star are the words "City of Houston, Texas." Within that circle is the city seal, which depicts a plow and a train locomotive with a star in its smoke. This seal dates from 1840, before the railroad had reached Houston, but the city anticipated great prosperity as a railroad shipping center and eventually this came to pass. The plow symbolizes Texas's agricultural wealth and Houston's contribution.

City of Houston flag

City of Dallas Flag

The site of Dallas was first settled in 1841 by John Neely Bryan as a trading post for Caddo and Cherokee Indians. French colonists from other parts of Texas began arriving at the site in the 1850s, and the community eventually was incorporated as a city in 1871. It was named after George Mifflin Dallas, American diplomat, and grew to be one of the largest inland cotton markets in the world.

The first flag of Dallas was adopted in 1916 but was not produced until 1954. The City Council decided Dallas needed a new flag, so a competition was held.

An appointed committee chose a design of a five-pointed white star on three stripes. The upper stripe is a wide red band, the center stripe is a narrow white band, and the lower stripe is a wide band in blue. Inside the star is the city seal—the Lone Star—on a gold background with the words "City of Dallas, Texas." The flag was officially adopted on February 13, 1967. A Lone Star design is featured on half the city flags in Texas.